AF237289

Tayala Léha
Third World War - a horror scenario...
CLOSER THAN WE THINK?!

Tayala Léha

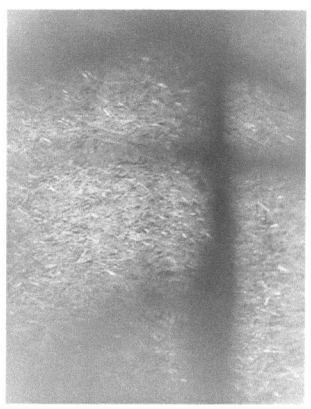

Third World War - a horror scenario...

CLOSER THAN WE THINK?!

Bibliographical information of the German National Library:
The German National Library lists this publication
in the German National Library; detailed bibliographical
information is available online at www.dnb.de.

Herstellung und Verlag:
BoD – Books on Demand, Norderstedt

ISBN 978-3-7557-0988-6

TABLE OF CONTENTS

Preface

I'm Tayala Léha, a healer and author with the gift of medium since birth.

I WANT TO WARN YOU!

In spring 2020, I was guided to the predictions of Alois Irlmaier. *My visions* coincided with a war that had already been predicted for many decades.

Has the time now come?

Ukraine – Russia.
Russia – Ukraine.

Armed conflicts up close.
A flood of refugees. Nobody wants to believe it, but it's true.

When referring to the Third World War, which may severely affect Germany in particular, Irlmaier said: "Nobody wants to believe it." Presumably here too, the first tanks would have to roll in before people realise that such things can happen against their wishes.

We hope it never comes to Russia attacking Western Europe, but... **THE WRITING IS ON THE WALL!**

Yours, Tayala Léha.

What are the signs of this war?

Irlmaier: "The war will break out when people are paying with small pieces of cardboard and talking with small, black boxes that also give them answers."

...credit cards and smartphones didn't exist in 1959.

***

The Left (political party) will **triumph** in Germany shortly before the war **but will not govern for long...**

***

The war will break out following a **very mild winter** and very **early and beautiful spring**.

***

Revolutions on the streets and **gradual inflation**…

***

"New laws will appear every day…".

***

The **global crisis** that immediately precedes the war…

What will cause the war?

An assassination attempt!

In the midsummer of year X, a "high-ranking person" will be murdered with a dagger by two assassins who manage to escape. This could happen at a peace conference in the Balkans.

Thereupon, Russia will attack the West (Western Europe) in the night, and small, yellow people will simultaneously invade Canada and the USA (Russian military alliance with China?!!).

Time of the war outbreak

"Oats will not yet be harvested, but wheat will be harvested." The oat harvest typically takes place in mid-August!

***

It will happen during the night of Friday to Saturday...between midnight and 2 am. It will be a rainy night...

***

I 'saw' the **13th of August**. Will that hold true?
In 2022, the 13th of August is in fact a Saturday!!

***

Irlmaier told his wife: "Once the assassination has taken place, you will have three days to cross the Rhine and head left towards Lake Constance. On the fourth day, it will be too late."

If the war breaks out during the night of Friday to Saturday, the assassination would presumably have to take place on a Tuesday or Wednesday.

***

Shortly before the war reaches Germany, **Turkey will invade Greece.** They will then travel around 100 km before they reach us...

Can I prepare?

Pack a **getaway backpack** with a good-quality water filter, important documents, cash and a small supply of precious metals (gold and silver). Pack food supplies. A cigarette lighter. Prepare a sleeping bag and mat. Take a handcart or bicycle. Cars will no longer work after the war.

***

Those fleeing should flee west of the Rhine or south of the Danube using side streets. The tanks will roll over anything on the motorways. Flee in good time! Once the Russians reach Germany, only two refugee trains will make it across the Danube towards the south. The third train will not make it.

How will the war evolve?

Everything will be destroyed between the Danube, Rhine and Elbe!

***

After the city of **Prague, northwards to a latitude of around 150 km,** death will prevail across a wide stretch until the large bay of water up to a Hanseatic City. Shortly after the outbreak of war, **drones are predicted to pour poison on this spot of Earth.** It will happen during the night. Everything and everyone will die instantly, *"even the worm 30 feet under the ground"* according to Irlmaier. This area will be inaccessible for over a year. Anyone who goes outside will die. This yellow dust will be dropped in order to cut the Russians off from their supplies.

***

None of the Russians that come over here will make it home.

A tidal wave will devastate northern France, Belgium, Holland, Denmark, northern Germany up to Hanover and Berlin, and the entire Rhine-Main region in Germany.

Half of England will be submerged and completely destroyed.

This tidal wave will be caused by a bomb dropped into the water by a plane between the mainland and England.

In general, the following will apply: **avoid all coastal regions up to around 300 above sea level!**

Will any places and countries be safe from the war?

In Germany, the region **south of the Danube and west of the Rhine** will be **relatively safe.**

However, major battles are predicted to take place in Cologne, Lyon and Strasbourg.

The Russians should not reach Spain via the Pyrenees. **Central Spain** is predicted to be a good choice, along with **the regions around Berchtesgaden, Lindau on Lake Constance and Allgäu in Germany.** Barring any civil unrest, it should be relatively tolerable there.

Thailand should remain unscathed by war according to local, ancient prophecies...

When and how will the war end?

A so-called **"three days of darkness" are thought to end the war,** which will last approximately 3 months, during a very cold night **in late autumn**. "When there is thunder and lightning outside, close the doors and windows **TIGHT**. Cover the windows with **black paper** and don't look outside. People who look out will die!".

Don't let anyone in. Avoid the deadly dust outside. Irlmaier: *"Anyone who inhales the dust will get a cramp and die."*

It will last three days and three nights. Darkness will prevail. The electricity will stop. Keep a candle light burning and pray - focus your spirit on God and hope. The sun will reappear on the fourth day, but in the West.

These three days of darkness will encompass the entire northern hemisphere and will be most deadly in Europe. It is also predicted in Thailand, but will be less deadly.
More people in Germany will die in these three days and nights than the total of the First and Second World Wars put together.

***

In order to survive these three days of darkness, you will need a **house** that can be completely sealed off.

Afterwards, any open water will be poisonous. Only drink the water from the tap.

Only dry food, such as flour, rice, pasta and tinned food will keep. Anything else (including in jars) will be poisonous afterwards. Anyone who eats it will die.

One source suggests wrapping a sheet of **aluminium foil** around jars for protection. This should fend off any radiation from the ground when the Earth's magnetic field collapses during the three days of darkness. Solar storms will then destroy all electronics. Multiple sheets of aluminium foil should also help here to protect technical devices against destruction.

What will happen after the war?

A **famine** will hit after the war. Therefore: **ensure you have at least a year's supply of food.**

At some point, food will be delivered via boats along the Danube again. Then, the famine will be over.

***

We will have to start over as we did 150 years previously - first **without electricity, electrics and electronics.**

***

The **monarchy** will flourish again.

***

A good period will then begin that is very different from before. *"One thousand years of peace"* will triumph.

I simply can't imagine it...

If someone had told us in 2017 that the coronavirus would turn everything on its head, that schools, shops, restaurants and all cultural facilities would be shut, that we would have to wear masks and socially distance, that we would live in a global state of emergency...who would have believed it? Probably nobody!
Just because we can't imagine something happening, that doesn't mean it will never happen.

Russia/Ukraine:
Would we have believed that war would break out in Ukraine? Would we have believed that women and children would be fleeing and that men would remain behind to fight? Everyone is horrified that this war is happening - so close...

However, according to the prophecy this war between Russia and Ukraine is just the beginning. You owe it to yourself and your loved ones to at least **be prepared** and take this matter seriously.

One prophecy still remains...

"Year of fire, flood and blood."

2020 was a very hot and dry year.

Floods happened in 2021...

2022 - blood is already flowing in Ukraine. And what will happen to us?

For 2022, my card reader sees **"a great deal of death in Germany and Europe!"**

Conclusion

"The war won't happen because I can't imagine it happening."

Everyone intuitively knows that this isn't the case. Anyone who believes the prophecy should prepare themselves. Anyone who is unprepared must face the consequences.

Take this booklet with you, carry it in your getaway bag and keep it to hand until midsummer 2022.

The greatest risk of a Third World War will happen from mid-July to mid-August, but not just here. Other countries will also be affected.

Feel free to read my other booklets, particularly **"3. Weltkrieg in 2022!"** This also contains other important tips…

I wish us all the very best and God's richest blessings, peace on Earth and love for all people, as...those who act with love will never start a war.

Tayala Léha

Book recommendations

Please read the comprehensive works of prophecy researcher Stephan Berndt!

These German-language books are available in German bookshops.

- "Countdown Weltkrieg 3.0 – Das Erscheinen der letzten Vorzeichen. Die Prophezeiungen und Visionen der Hellseher erfüllen sich."
  ISBN 978-3-86445-407-3
- "3 Tage im Spätherbst. Wie Hellseher weltweit seit Jahrhunderten eine 3-tägige Finsternis für unsere Zeit vorhersehen."
  ISBN 978-3-86445-714-2
- "REFUGIUM. Sichere Gebiete nach Alois Irlmaier und anderen Sehern."
  ISBN 978-3-946433-30-9

...more from Tayala Léha:

This book is also available in a German printout.

„Horrorszenario 3. Weltkrieg...
Näher, als wir glauben?!"
ISBN 978-3-7526-8745-3

AND... another German printout from Tayala Léha:

„3. Weltkrieg in 2022!
Was ich BISHER nicht wusste..."
978-3-7557-5549-4

These books are available in bookstores in Germany, Austria and Switzerland as well as in India, China, South Korea, Brazil, England, Australia, Canada and the USA.